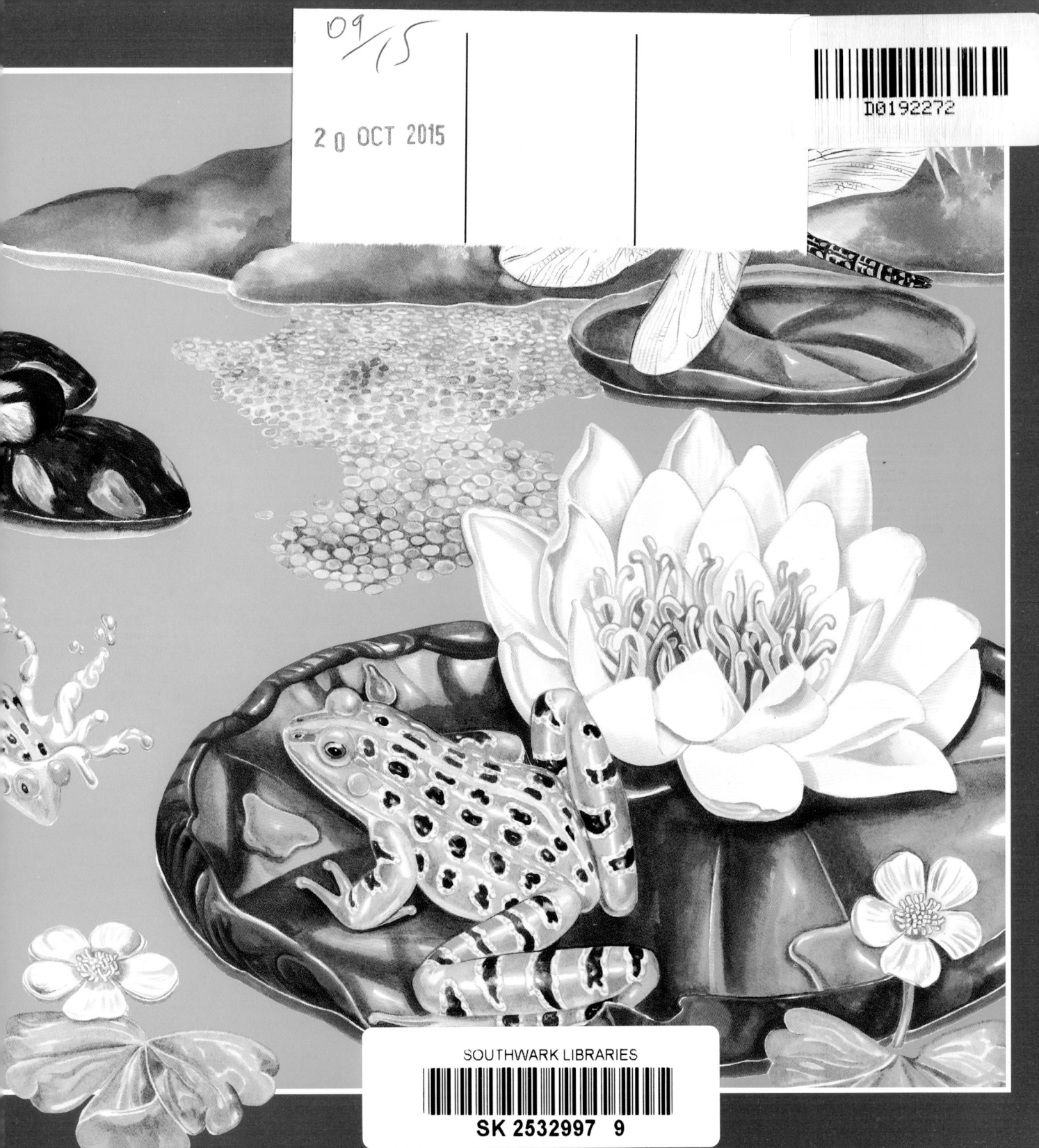

# From Tadpole to Frog
## Notes and activities by Karina Law, author and educational consultant

Each book in the *Lifecycles* series traces a story of growth and change.
Here are some ideas of how to get the most of *From Tadpole to Frog*:

## Responding to the text

Once you have read through the book with children, ask open-ended questions to assess their comprehension.

- Can they think of other creatures with webbed feet?
- What do tadpoles use to breathe under water? Which other animals use gills to breathe? What do frogs use to breathe?
- Talk about the way in which a frog uses its long sticky tongue to catch insects. Can they think of other animals that catch food in this way?

## Features of non-fiction texts

Challenge children to locate specific information in the book using the contents page (page 6) or the index (page 29). Where would they look to find out how tadpoles and frogs breathe? Where would they look to find out about webbed feet? Which page would they turn to if they wanted to read about tadpoles?

Look at the glossary of frog words on page 28. How many of these words were the children already familiar with? Which words are new to them? Why are the words in alphabetical order?

## Language and literacy

Ask children to describe a frog's appearance. How do they imagine a frog would feel if they were to hold one in their hands? What might frogspawn feel like?

Look for poems, rhymes and stories about frogs to share with the child. For example, *Five little Speckled Frogs*; *The Frog Prince*.

'Lifecycles' is a frequently studied topic with many cross-curricular links. Children can use *From Tadpole to Frog* as a starting point for thinking about other lifecycles. They could watch the different stages of a flowering plant, such as a sunflower, as it grows from a seed into a flower and then produces more seeds to grow new plants.

These are some suggestions for continuing the learning process through practical, fun activities.

## Lifecycle wheel

This activity will help to reinforce children's understanding of a lifecycle.

You will need thin white card, a ruler, a paper fastener, scissors, a pencil, felt-tip pens.

*What to do:*
1. Draw and cut out two circles of equal size from the card, with a diameter of about 20 cm.
2. Draw two straight lines across one of the circles, dividing it into four equal sections.
3. Using the illustrations on pages 26 and 27, ask the children to draw each of the following life-stages of the frog: frogspawn, tadpole at 1 week, tadpole at 9 weeks, fully grown frog. Draw one life-stage in each segment, in a clockwise direction.
4. Cut out a quarter segment from the top circle to create a 'window', taking care not to cut too near the centre.
5. Place the second circle over the circle with the drawings. Fix the two circles together by pushing a paper fastener through the centre.
6. Decorate the top circle and show the children how to turn the 'wheel' to reveal the different stages in the lifecycle of a frog in sequence.

## Frog collage

Make a collage of a frog pond together. Talk with the children about the different materials they use to create their picture. What words can they think of to describe the different colours and textures?

You will need a sheet of thin card, glue, bubble wrap, a black permanent marker pen, paints or felt-tip pens, glue, 2 buttons or sequins, recycled materials (e.g. fabric, wool, foil, coloured cellophane, crepe paper, tissue paper, sweet wrappers, gummed paper).

*What to do:*
1. Using the sheet of card for a background, help the children to plan a frog pond scene.
2. Use bubble wrap to create frogspawn, drawing a black dot in the centre of each bubble with a marker pen.
3. Create reeds and underwater plants using paints or recycled materials.
4. Create a frog using the paints, felt-tip pens or recycled materials. Stick on buttons or sequins for eyes.

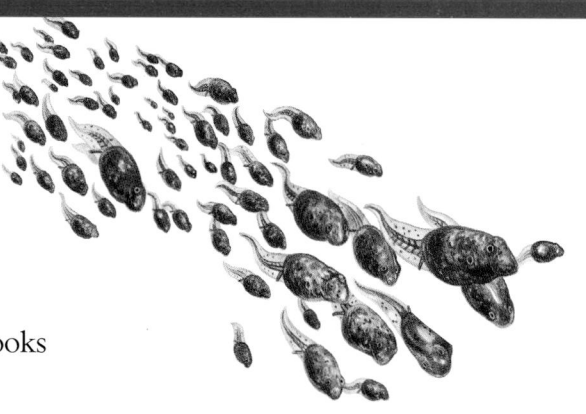

This edition published in 2014

Editor  April McCroskie
Language Consultant  Prue Goodwin
Natural History Consultant  Dr Gerald Legg

David Stewart has written many non-fiction books for children. He lives in Brighton.

Carolyn Scrace is a graduate of Brighton College of Art, specialising in design and illustration. She has worked in animation, advertising and children's fiction. She is a major contributor to the popular *Worldwise* series.

Professor Viv Edwards is professor of Language in Education and director of the National Centre for Language and Literacy at the University of Reading.

Dr Gerald Legg holds a doctorate in zoology from Manchester University. He is the Keeper of the Booth Museum of Natural History in Brighton.

David Salariya was born in Dundee, Scotland, where he studied illustration and printmaking, specialising in book design in his postgraduate year, he has designed and created many new series of children's books for publishers in the UK and overseas.

ISBN: 978 1 4451 2952 5
Dewey Classification: 597.8


Printed in China

An SBC Book conceived, edited and designed by
The Salariya Book Company
25 Marlborough Place Brighton BN1 1UB

A CIP catalogue record for this book is available from the British Library

First published in the UK by
Franklin Watts
338 Euston Road,
London, NW1 3BH

Franklin Watts Australia
Level 17/207 Kent Street,
Sydney, NSW 2000

Franklin Watts is a division of
Hachette Children's Books,
an Hachette UK company
www.hachette.co.uk

# lifecycles

# From Tadpole to Frog

Written by David Stewart
Illustrated by Carolyn Scrace

Created & Designed by David Salariya

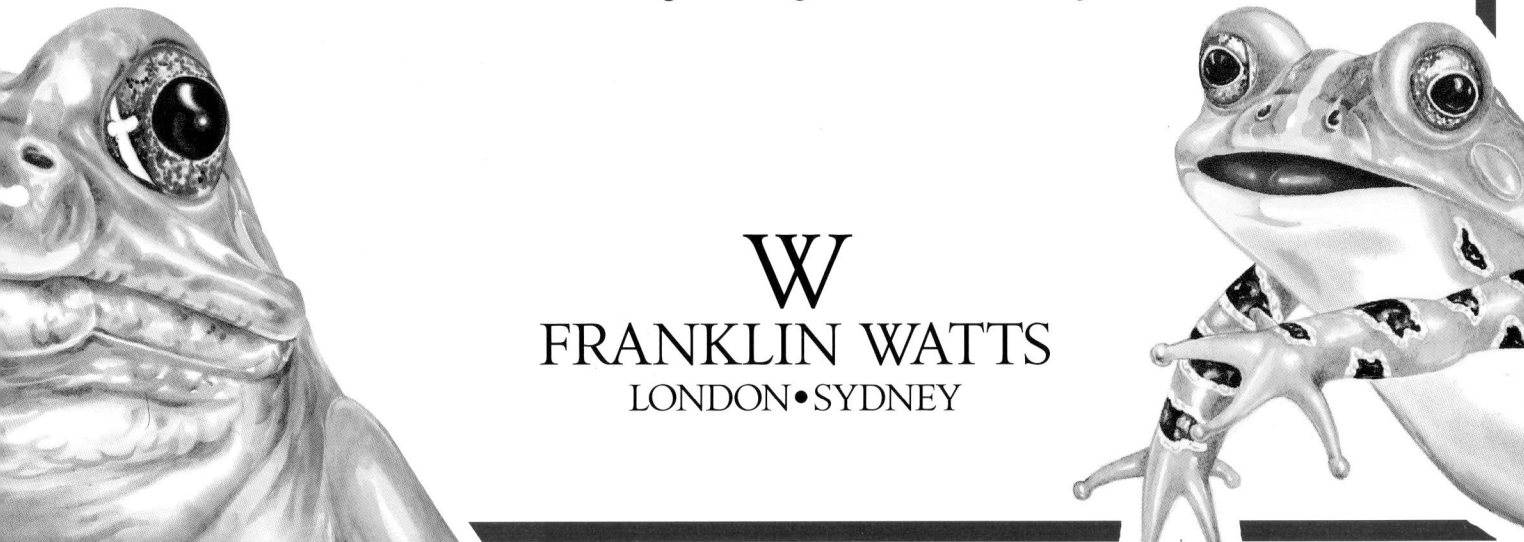

## W
### FRANKLIN WATTS
LONDON • SYDNEY

Introduction            7
What is a frog?         8
Frog-spawn             10
Tadpoles              12
Eating food           14
Arms and legs         16
Out of the water      18
Froglets              20
Danger                22
Mating call           24
Frog facts            26
Frog words            28
Index                 29

 A frog begins life as an egg. A tadpole hatches from the egg. The tadpole grows into a froglet, and finally into a frog. In this book you can see this amazing life cycle unfold.

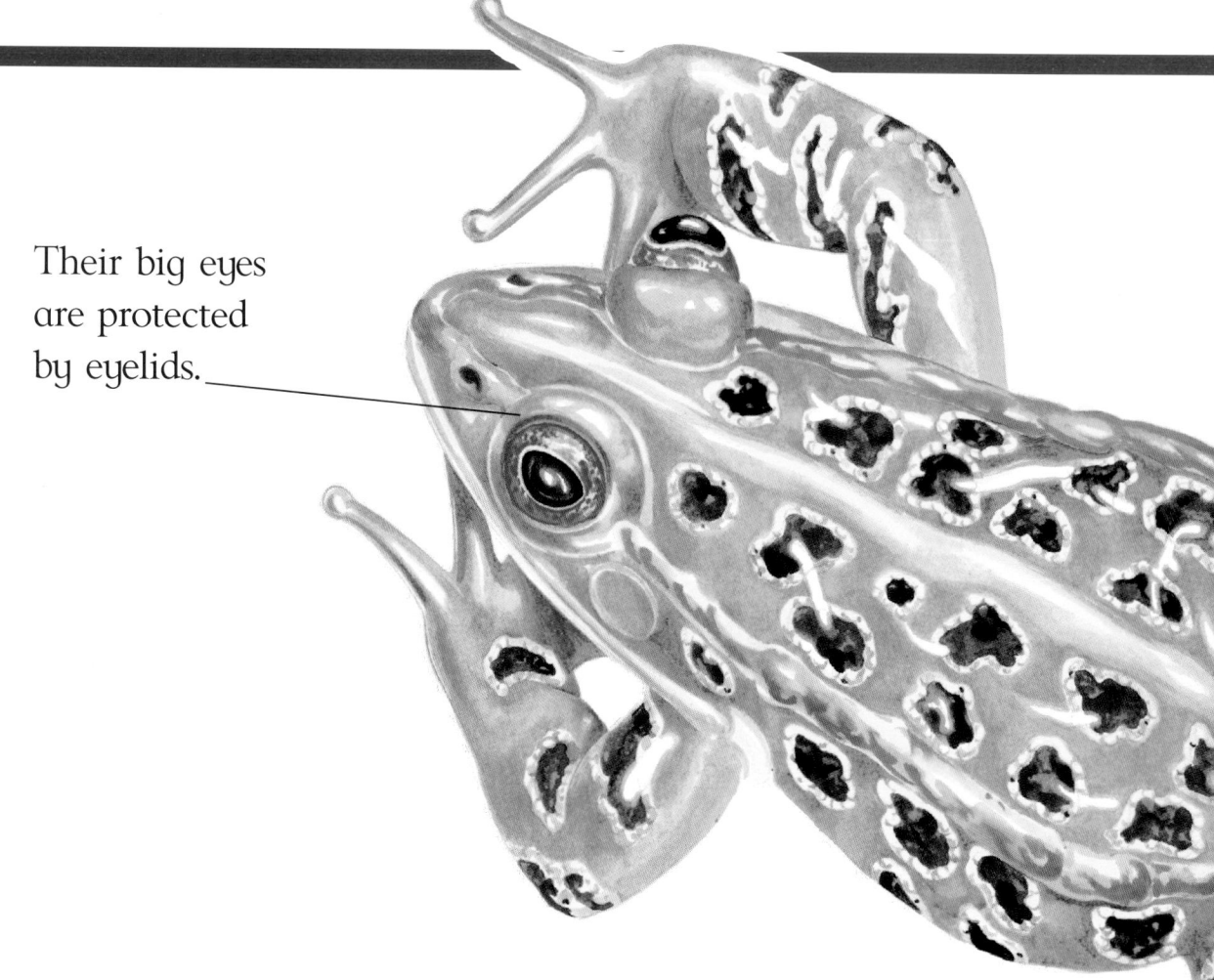

Their big eyes
are protected
by eyelids.

Frogs live most of the time
in or near water. Their strong
back legs, with webbed feet,
are good for swimming.

Frogs can live
in water and
on land.
Animals that
can do this are
called amphibians.

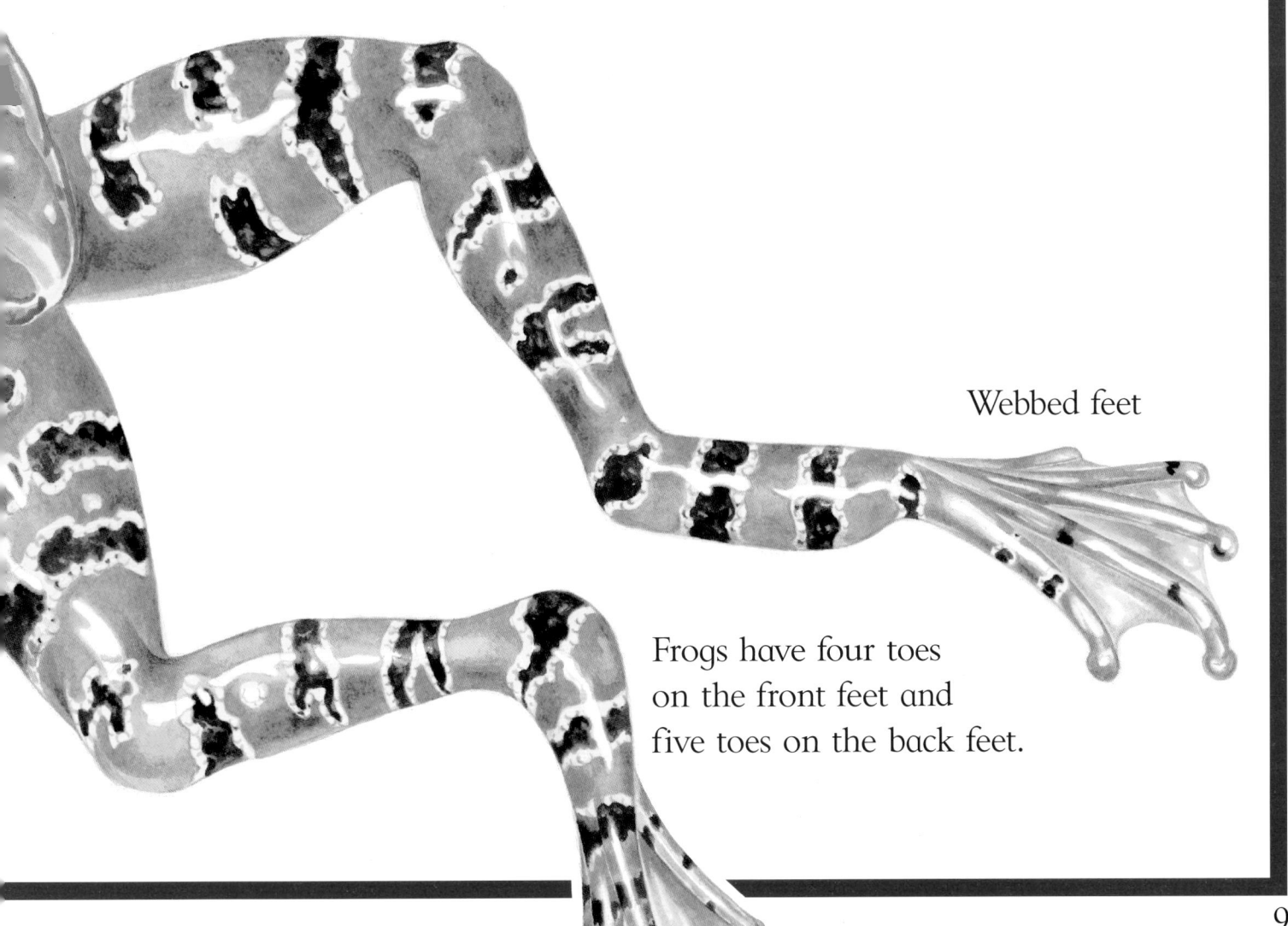

Webbed feet

Frogs have four toes
on the front feet and
five toes on the back feet.

In spring the female frog lays eggs, and the male frog covers them with a liquid called sperm. The eggs are fertilized by the sperm and begin to grow.

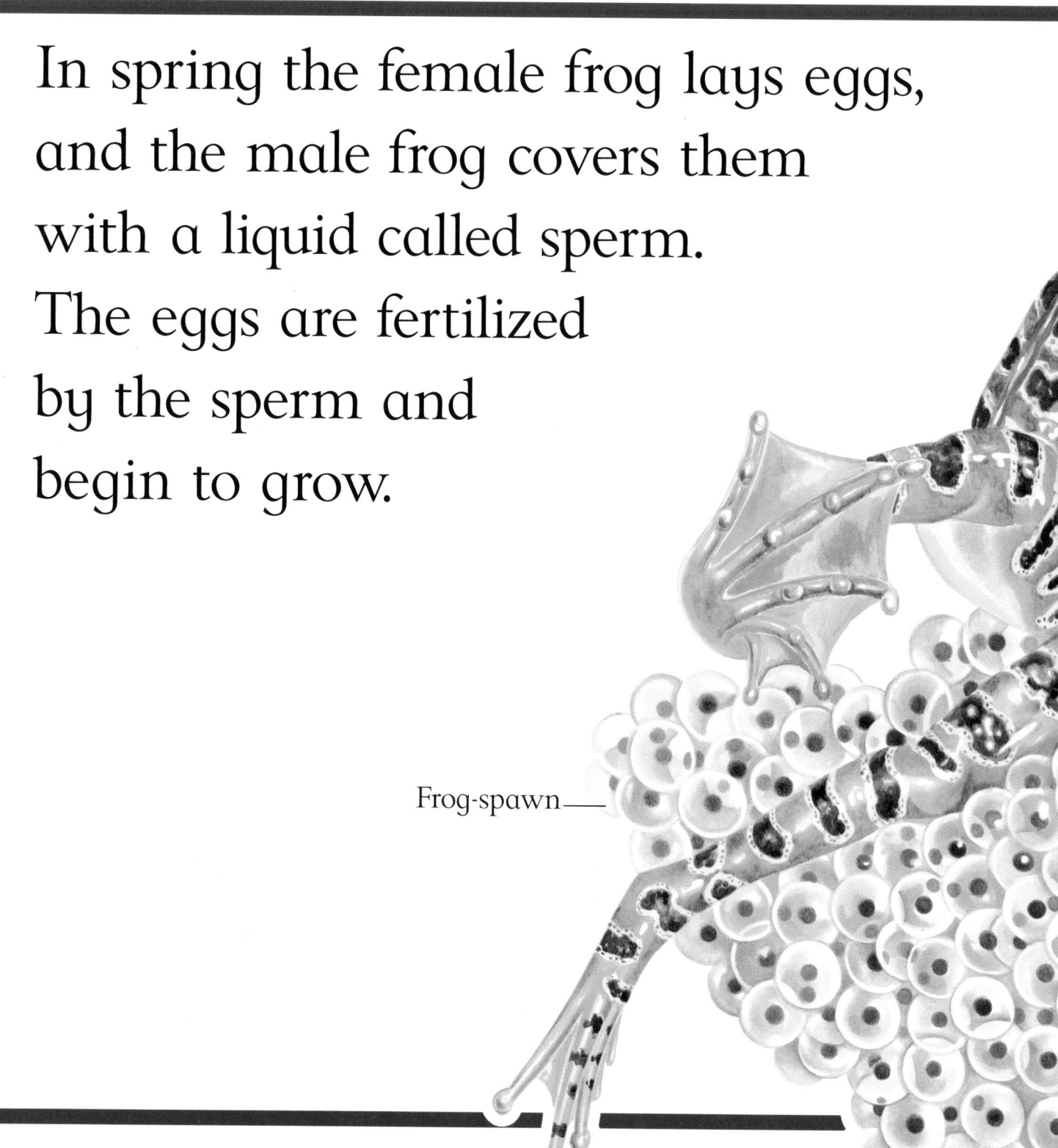

Frog-spawn ———

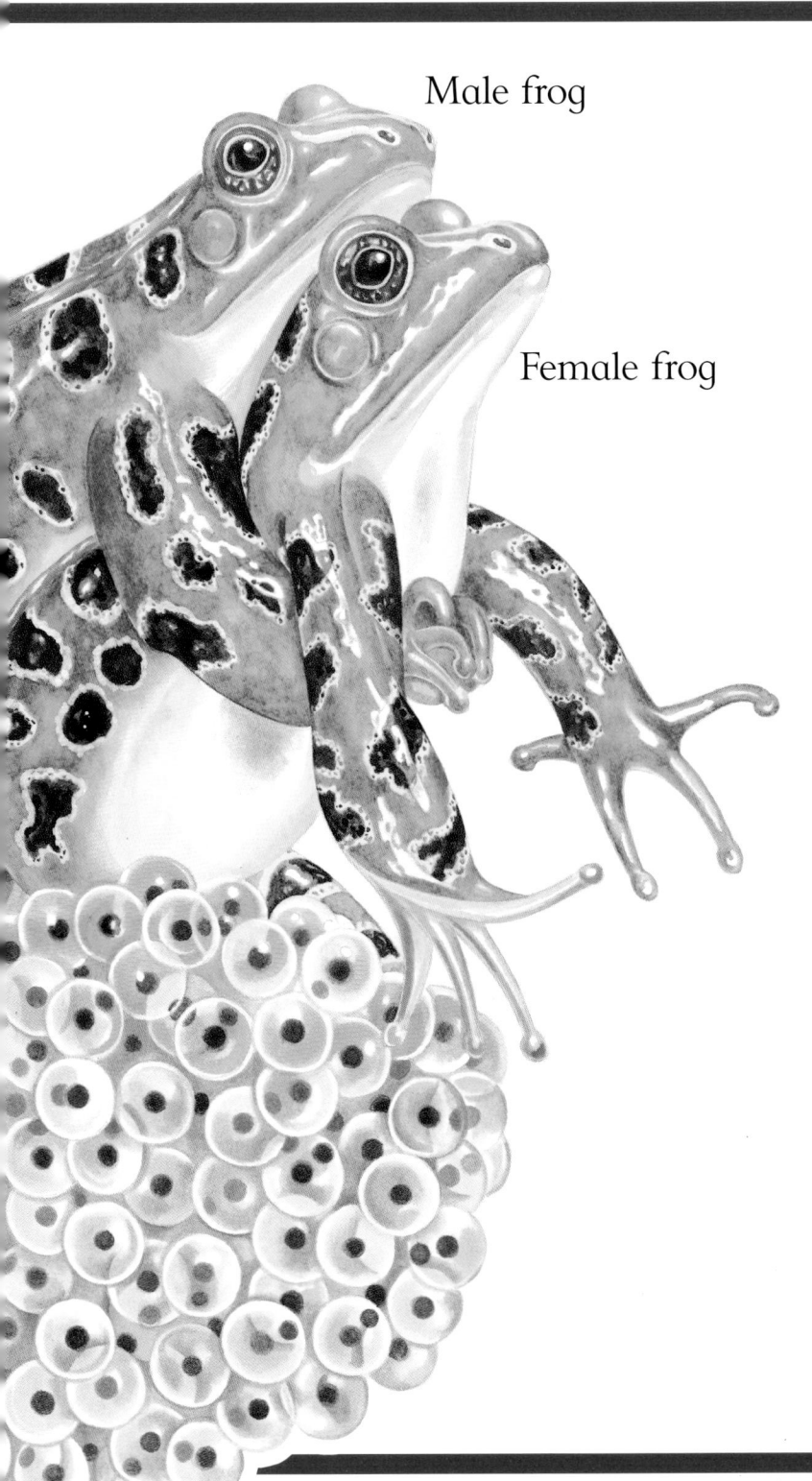

Male frog

Female frog

The eggs stick together to form frog-spawn. The frog-spawn floats to the top of the water.

Each egg grows
inside a ball
of jelly.

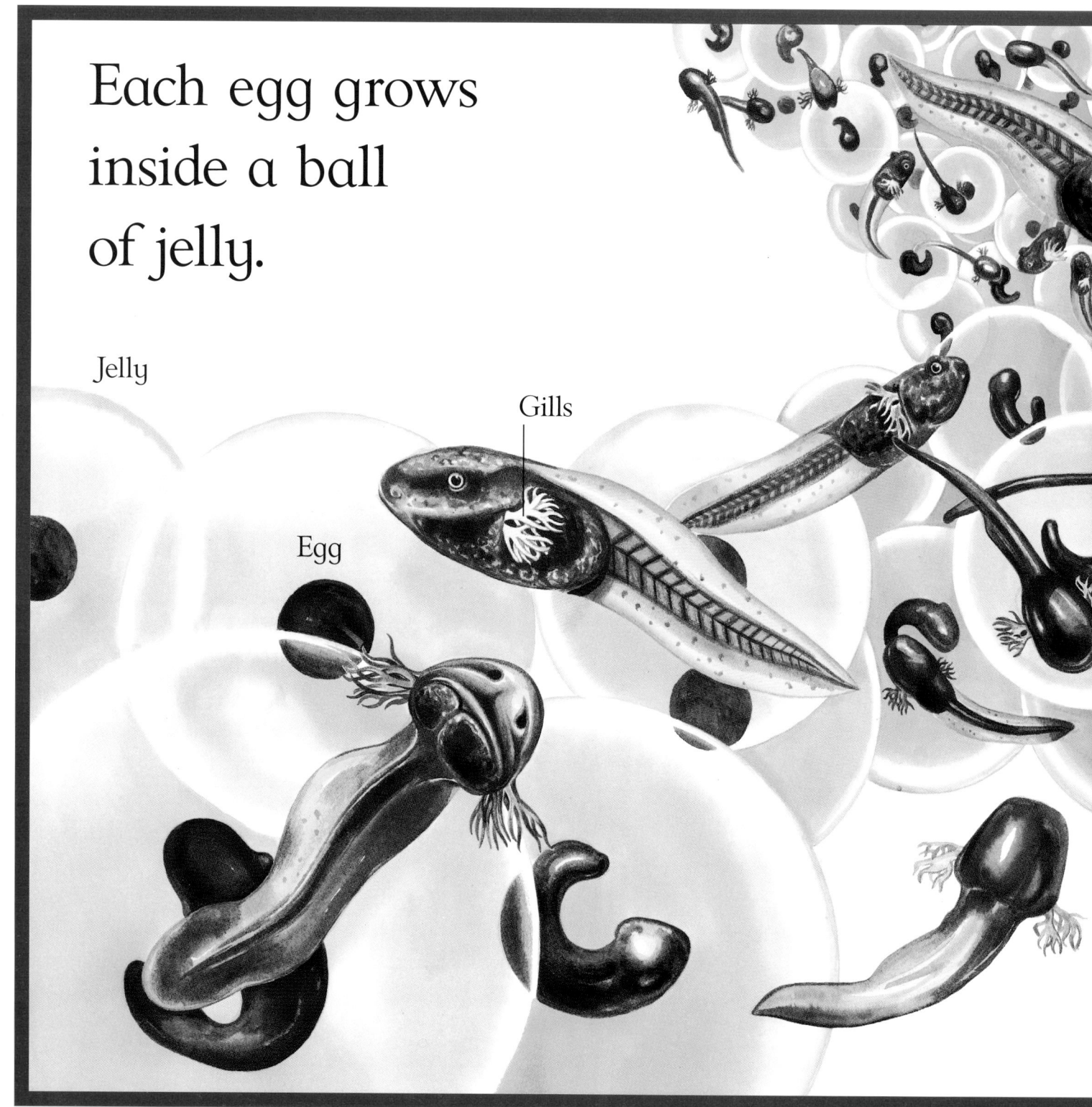

Jelly

Gills

Egg

Tadpole

A few days later
the tadpoles hatch out.
They live under water
and breathe through
their gills.

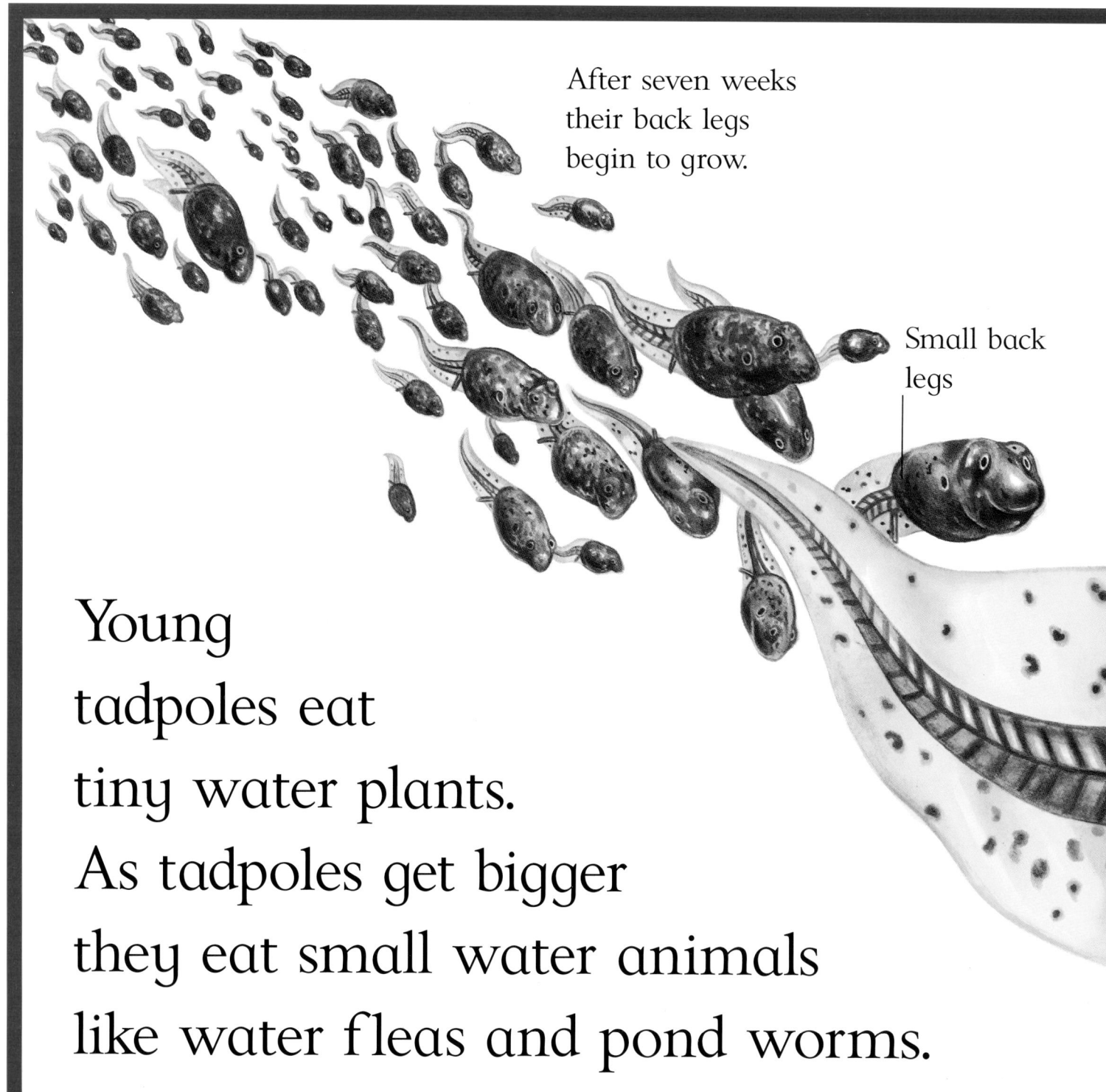

After seven weeks their back legs begin to grow.

Small back legs

Young
tadpoles eat
tiny water plants.
As tadpoles get bigger
they eat small water animals
like water fleas and pond worms.

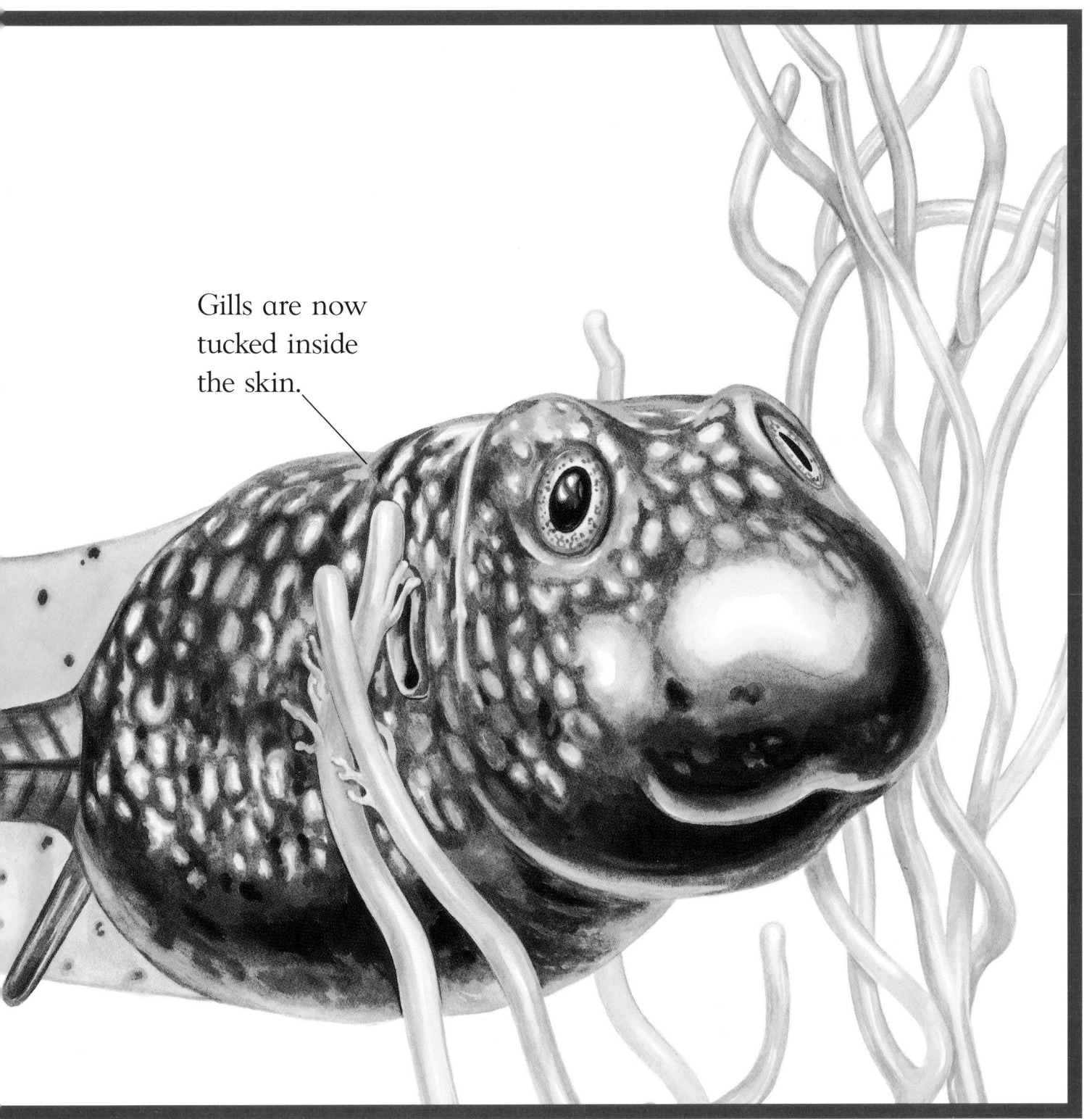

Gills are now
tucked inside
the skin.

The tail shrinks.
After nine weeks
front legs grow
near where the gills
used to be.

Before, the tadpoles used their gills to breathe. Now they use their lungs.

After twelve weeks
the tadpoles can
swim to the surface
of the water and
breathe in air.

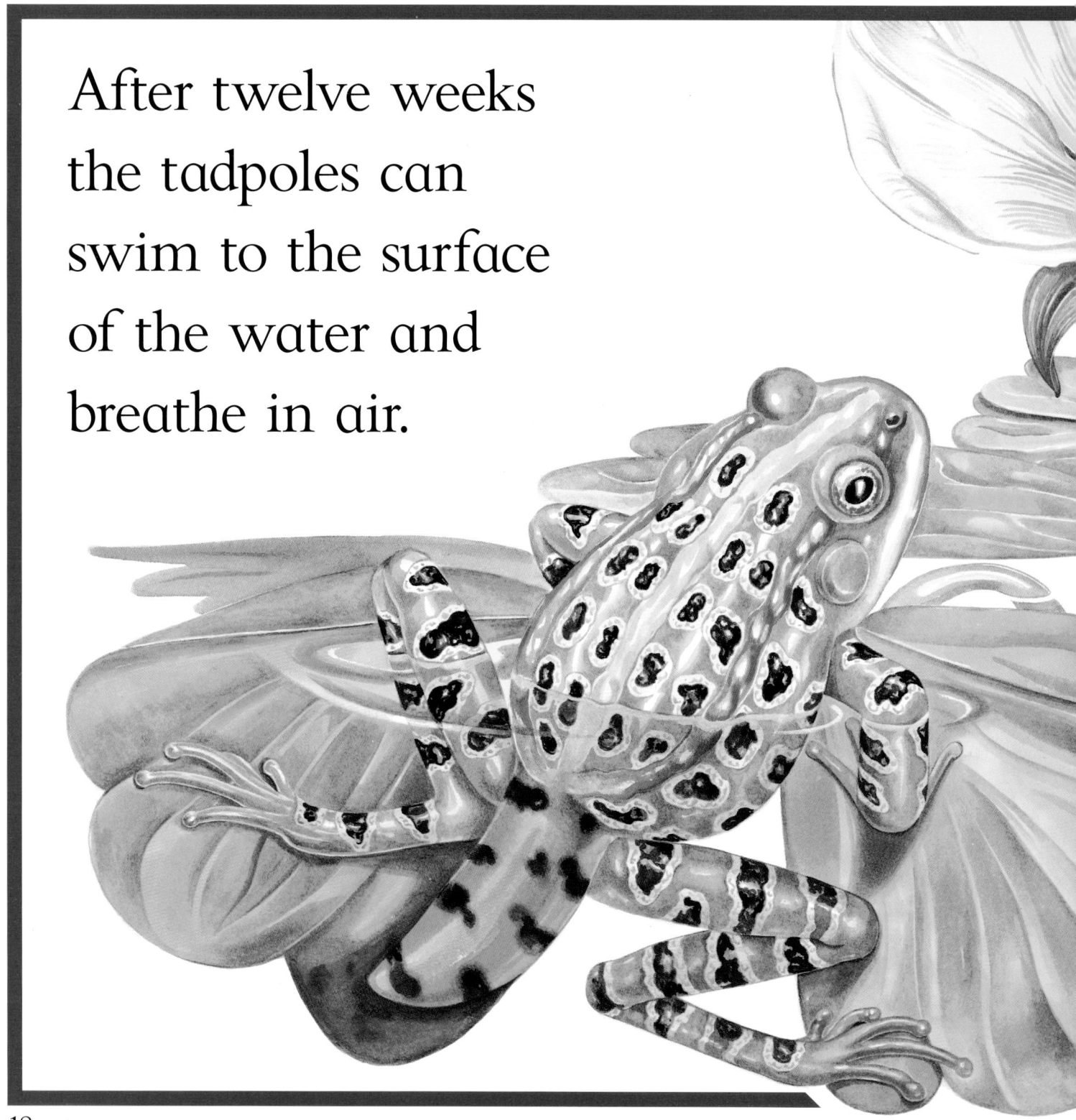

Only the back legs
are used for
swimming.

Webbed toes help
the young frog
to swim faster.

After three months
the tadpoles have
become young frogs,
and are called froglets.
Frogs are amphibians.
This means that
they can live
in or out of water.
They have long,
sticky tongues that are
good for catching insects.

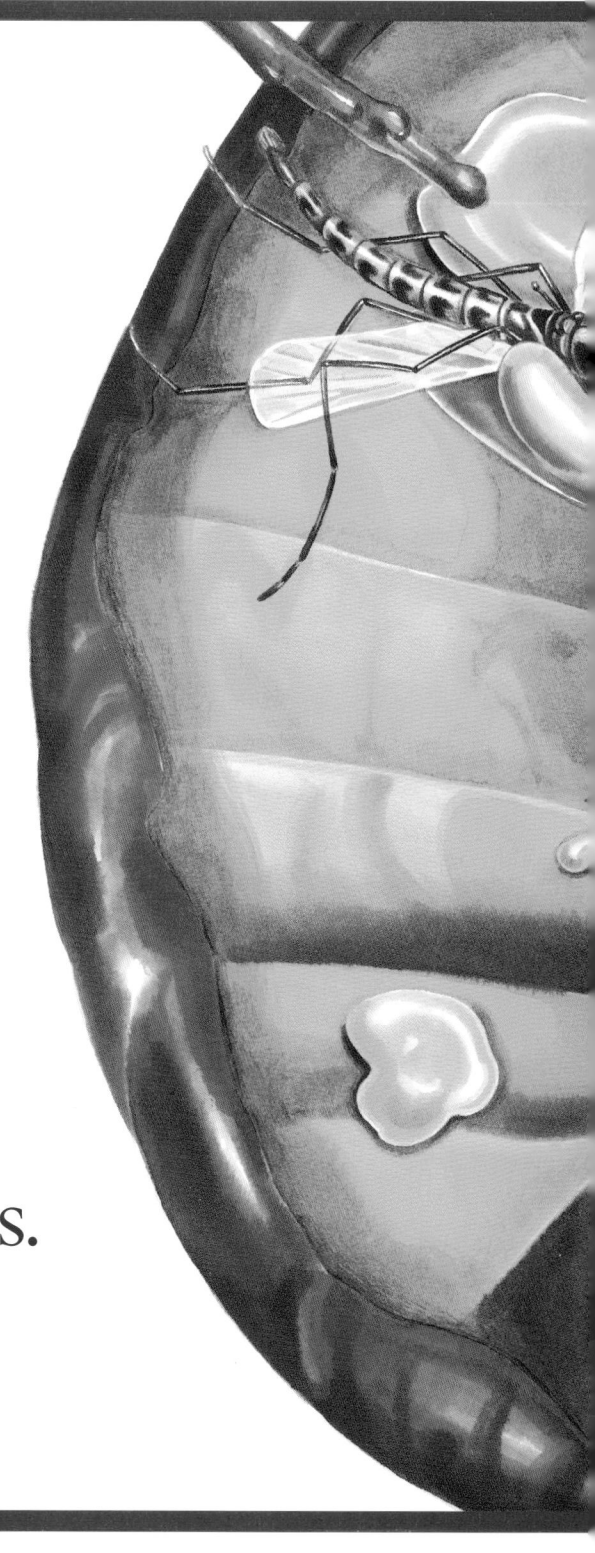

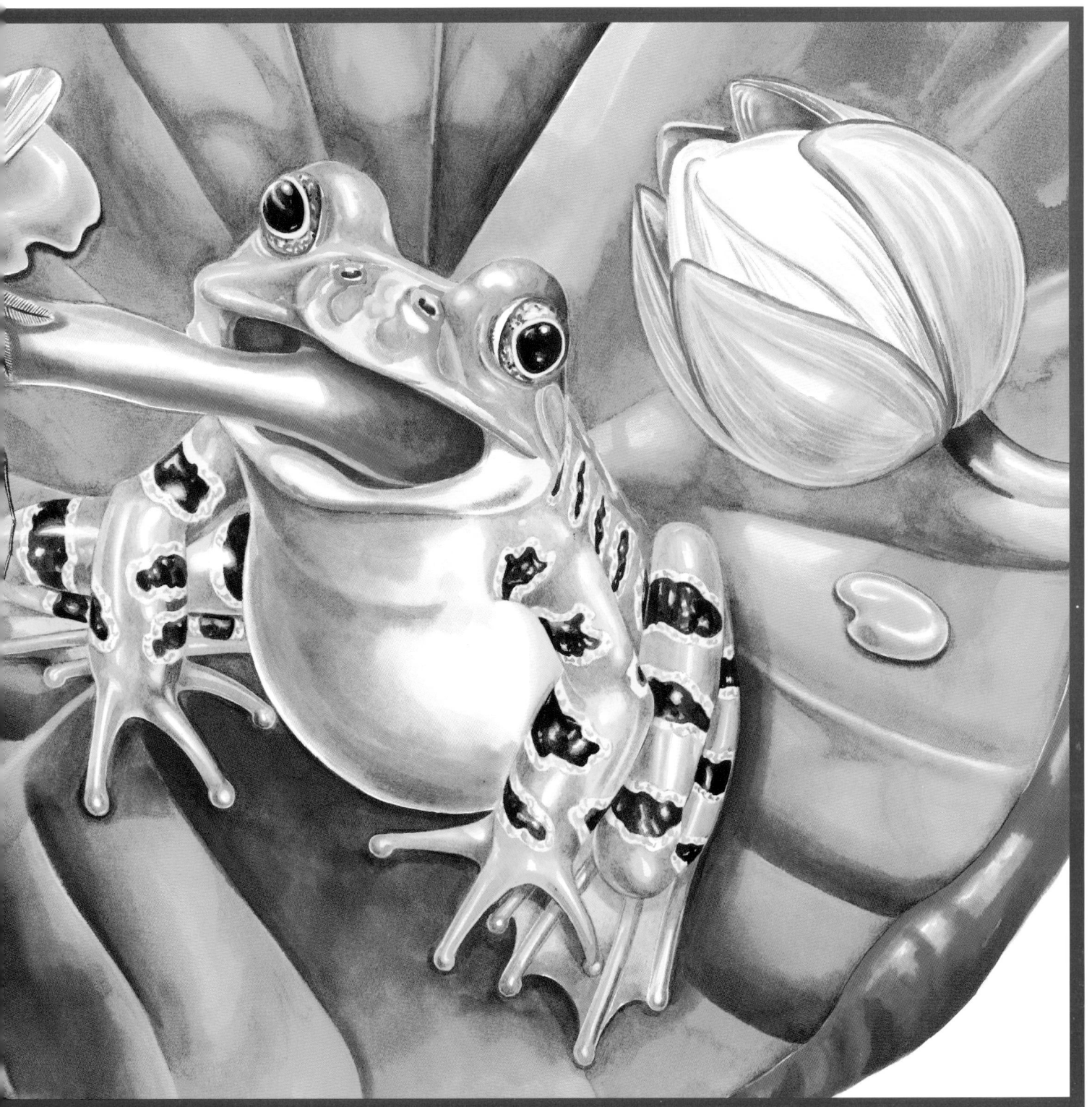

Froglets face many dangers.
Some animals like to catch
and eat them.

Frogs grow up to look like their parents.
When she is three years old,
the female frog will lay eggs.

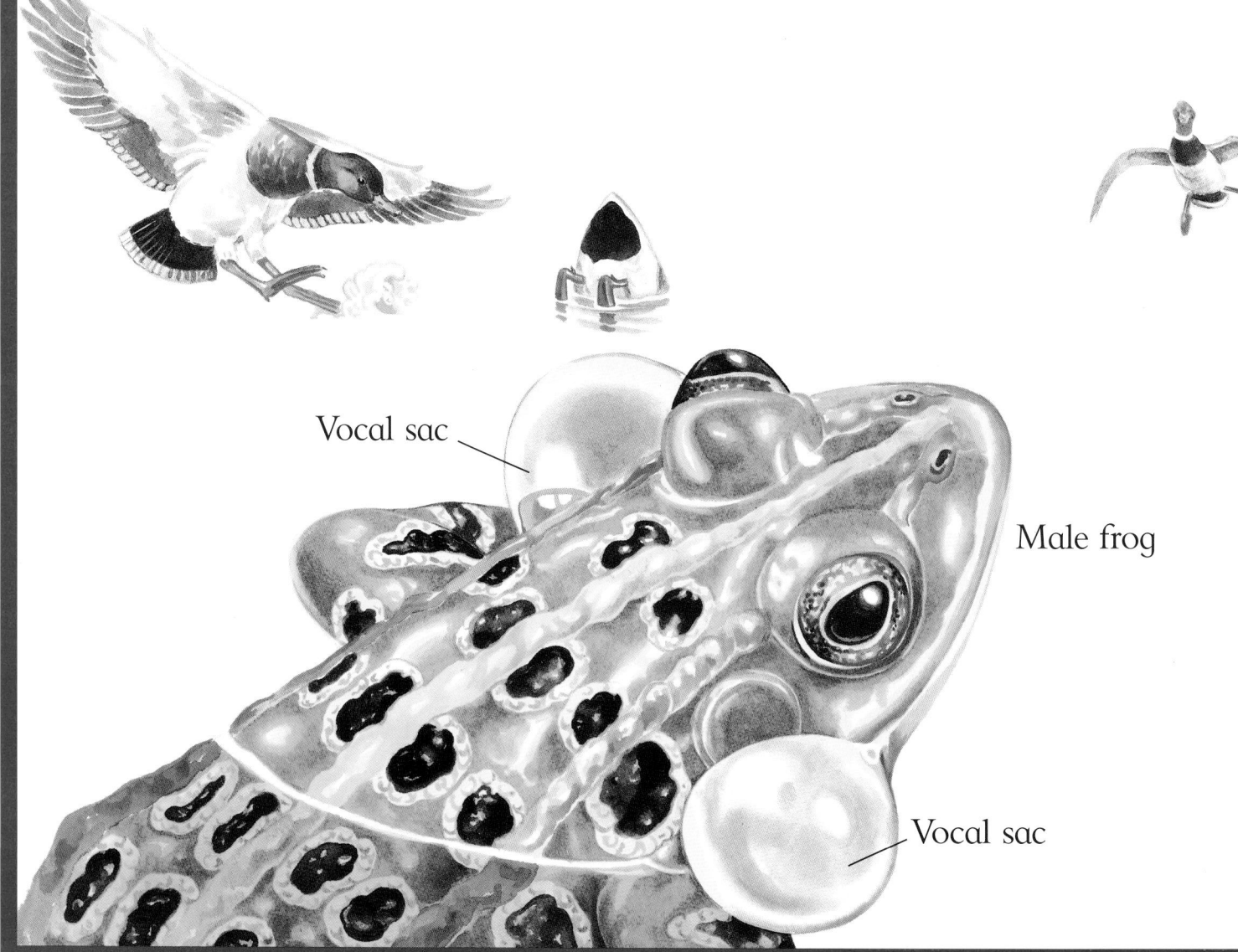

Vocal sac

Male frog

Vocal sac

The male frog
tries to attract
the female.

Female frog

He expands his vocal sacs
and sings to her.

# Frog facts

A frog is an amphibian. Amphibians begin their lives in water.

The smallest amphibian is an arrow poison frog from Cuba. It is about one centimetre long.

Frogs are cold-blooded creatures. Their body temperature changes with the temperature around them.

Frogs have smooth, wet skin. Toads have dry, bumpy skin.

Some frogs live in trees. There are over 300 species of tree frog.

Tree frogs have large webbed feet. This helps them leap between trees.

A species of frog called the White's tree frog has disc-shaped toes that act like suckers. These help it to cling to branches.

Tree frogs live on insects and on the water that collects in leaves.

## The growth of a frog

In the pictures below you can see the way a frog grows. First, the frog's egg hatches into a tadpole. Next, a tadpole becomes a young froglet. Finally, a froglet grows into a frog.

| Egg | 1 week | 7 weeks | 9 weeks | 12 weeks | 14 weeks |

In the tropical forests of Asia, the flying frog can "fly" for about 14 metres. It has big webbed feet that act like birds' wings.

A rare frog from New Zealand lives far from water. It does not have tadpoles. Small frogs emerge straight from the eggs.

Arrow poison frogs are found in Central and South America. They produce the most lethal poisons of any creature.

The largest frog is the goliath frog of western Africa. It can grow to a length of about one metre and weighs over three kilograms.

20 weeks

Fully grown

# Frog words

**Amphibians**
Creatures able to live in water or on land. They begin their lives in water.

**Expand**
Make bigger.

**Froglet**
A young frog.

**Fertilization**
When an egg and sperm join together. The egg and sperm will become a baby.

**Frog-spawn**
The sticky eggs that float on the surface of the water. Tadpoles hatch from frog-spawn.

**Gills**
These are needed by creatures to breathe under water. They are outside the body.

**Lungs**
These are needed by creatures to breathe air. They are inside the body.

**Species**
A group of animals that look alike, live in the same way and produce young that do the same.

**Sperm**
The liquid from the male that joins the egg from the female to produce a baby.

**Tadpole**
The small creature that hatches from a frog's egg.

**Vocal sac**
The part of a frog's throat that allows it to make a croaking sound.

**Webbed feet**
Feet with stretched skin between the toes. Webbed feet help frogs to swim.

# Index

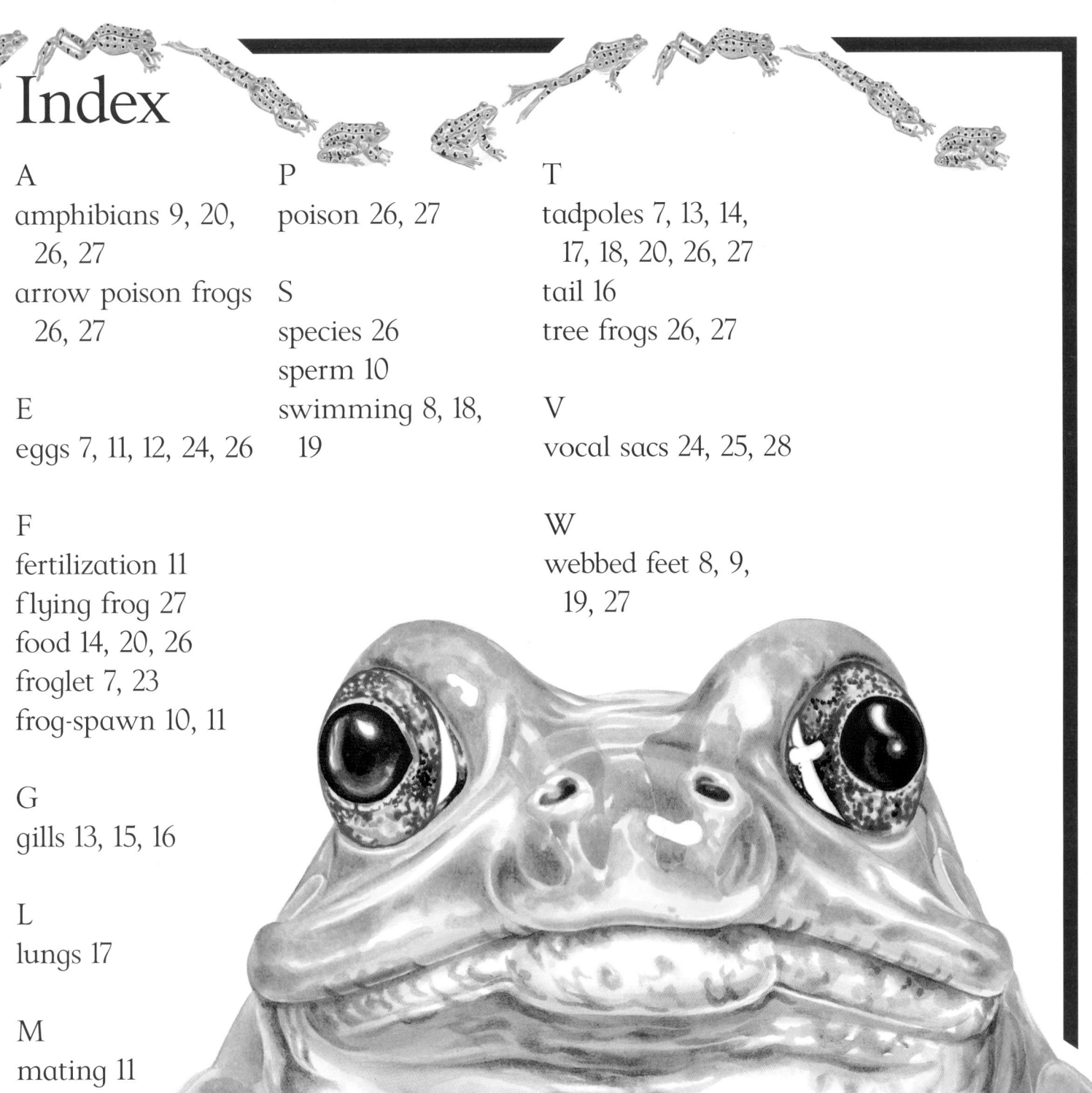

**A**

amphibians 9, 20, 26, 27

arrow poison frogs 26, 27

**E**

eggs 7, 11, 12, 24, 26

**F**

fertilization 11

flying frog 27

food 14, 20, 26

froglet 7, 23

frog-spawn 10, 11

**G**

gills 13, 15, 16

**L**

lungs 17

**M**

mating 11

**P**

poison 26, 27

**S**

species 26

sperm 10

swimming 8, 18, 19

**T**

tadpoles 7, 13, 14, 17, 18, 20, 26, 27

tail 16

tree frogs 26, 27

**V**

vocal sacs 24, 25, 28

**W**

webbed feet 8, 9, 19, 27